HR-AUTHORIZED WAYS TO TELL COWORKERS THEY'RE DUMB

Packed with Witty Jokes, Humor And HR-Approved Office Pranks

Jim Office

ISBN: ISBN: 979-8-89095-045-1

INTRODUCTION

We all have that One Coworker. You know the one.

They might be a lovely person. They might bring a breath of fresh air to the office. They might be the first one there in the morning, or the first one to bring you a cup of coffee or tell you about their weekend.

But when it comes to actually doing the job you're there for, they perhaps don't quite pull their full weight. Or, put less tactfully, they're just plain dumb.

You can't tell them that in the office, of course. These days, we need to be careful and professional in what we say and how we act around our colleagues, no matter how doltish, flea-brained, and lunk-headed they may be!

So if you were just to call them out for their stupidity, HR would be on your back and in your inbox as quick as a flash.

No, to let them know they're not playing with the full deck or not quite the sharpest pencil in the drawer, you need to be more skilful in your choice of words.

You need to craft an insult so cunning and so vague that the person you're actually insulting doesn't even realize it's an insult in the first place! That way, you can get what you need to say off your chest, without HR ever batting an eye.

And that's where this book comes in.

This is a collection of *HR-Authorized* Ways To Tell Coworkers They're Dumb*. Inside these pages, we've assembled dozens of different ways to call out your coworkers' stupidity without ever truly getting caught doing so.

Along the way here too, we have plenty of other office fun and games to keep you busy, including jokes, memes, one-liners, and even prank ideas so you can get back at that One Coworker that we're all talking about here.

So let's get started—quick, before someone from HR notices...

---

* *Please be aware that HR may or may not actually have approved these insults, so use them at your discretion. Hey, we did warn you.*

#1
HR-APPROVED INSULT

"That's a good point. And I would agree with you, except then we'd both be wrong."

Did your coffee mug just tell you that you have a nice tie on today?
Sure, the coffee here is complimentary.
My careers advisor told me to follow my dreams.
What did you do, go back to bed?

OFFICE PRANKS

THE MONDAY MORNING COFFEE PRANK

First thing on a Monday morning, everyone in the office needs a cup of coffee, right?

So, why not make sure you're the first one to arrive there at the start of the working week (yeah—it's a big ask, we know), then sneak into the break room and start brewing up the first pot of coffee before anyone else arrives.

Only this time, make sure the first pot of the week is decaf!

How long before your coworkers realize they're not getting their usual buzz of a Monday morning?

How long before someone goes back for a second cup? Then a third, then a fourth—still waiting for that caffeine hit that never comes?

The only thing you have to worry about then, is whether or not to admit the prank ... or just wait and see if anyone works it out before you, after the eyelids start getting droopy and the brains start to fog over just after midday!

Preparing for a Zoom meeting
when you're working from home and own a cat.

#2
HR-APPROVED INSULT

"They set themselves enormously high standards and are absolutely consistent in not meeting them."

Why haven't you tidied the stationery cupboard?

I'm sorry, I draw the line with rulers.

Did you hear about the company that makes yardsticks?

They're not making them any longer.

OFFICE PRANKS

THE VOICE-OPERATED TECHNOLOGY PRANK

Technology is moving faster and faster than ever before these days, and new devices and ingenious tech breakthroughs seem to be happening ever more frequently.

So why not take advantage of that (as well as taking advantage of your most gullible coworkers) with a little prank involving the copier room?

Don't have a photocopier in your office? No problem. This prank works with any kind of device that people need to use on a regular basis around the office space—whether that's a printer, the coffee machine, the water cooler, the elevator ... hey, take your pick!

So. Sneak into the office early one day and fix up the most professional-looking sign you can beside the newest-looking device you can find, saying that the technology has been updated, and this device now works on voice-operated commands.

Then, just sit back and wait for your first victim to walk up to the copier, place their document under the hood, notice your sign and start barking their instructions out as loudly and clearly as they can!

OFFICE WISDOM

"No, no, I don't just consider you a coworker.

You don't do any work."

#3
HR-APPROVED INSULT

"He's absolutely foolproof.
He provides proof of the existence of fools."

Why do I need to file an incident report for my coffee?
It's been mugged!
What has plenty of keys but can't open anything?
Your keyboard.

OFFICE PRANKS

QUOTE-OF-THE-DAY PRANK

Who doesn't love a bit of Monday morning inspiration?

You might have a work email that does this already, of course, in which case you can just piggyback on the success of that. But if your office is one of the lucky ones that has yet to get into the weekly motivational email game, then it's going to fall to you to start it off. Only with a delightful prankish twist.

Tell everyone in the office that you're going to start sending a daily email around the office with a motivational quote for everyone to ponder over. The quotes can be as legitimate as you want—or, of course, you can make up your own madcap ones. The fun comes when you start telling people who said them.

"There's no such thing as a bad Monday, only a bad Monday attitude," you might like to tell everyone, before attributing that quote to someone completely unlikely. Mother Theresa of Calcutta, perhaps. Joseph Stalin, maybe. Joan of Arc might be another good one.

"The only thing that saps your time at work is your desire not to work harder than you know you truly could." Did you know that's a quote legitimately attributed to St. Francis of Assisi? No? Well, that's because he never said anything of the sort.

How long before your coworkers get wind of your game and start questioning the legitimacy of your quotes, your motivational aphorisms, and the random people from history you're attributing them to? A day? A week? Can you go undiscovered for an entire month? In the words of, oh, I don't know... King Henry VIII of England, "Verily, all good office workspaces need an office prankster."

OFFICE WISDOM

"The boss told me
I could leave early
so long as I made
up the time.

So I told him it was
seventy-two past
fourteen."

#4

HR-APPROVED INSULT

No, no, you're not the dumbest person in the office. Clive has brought his dog in today."

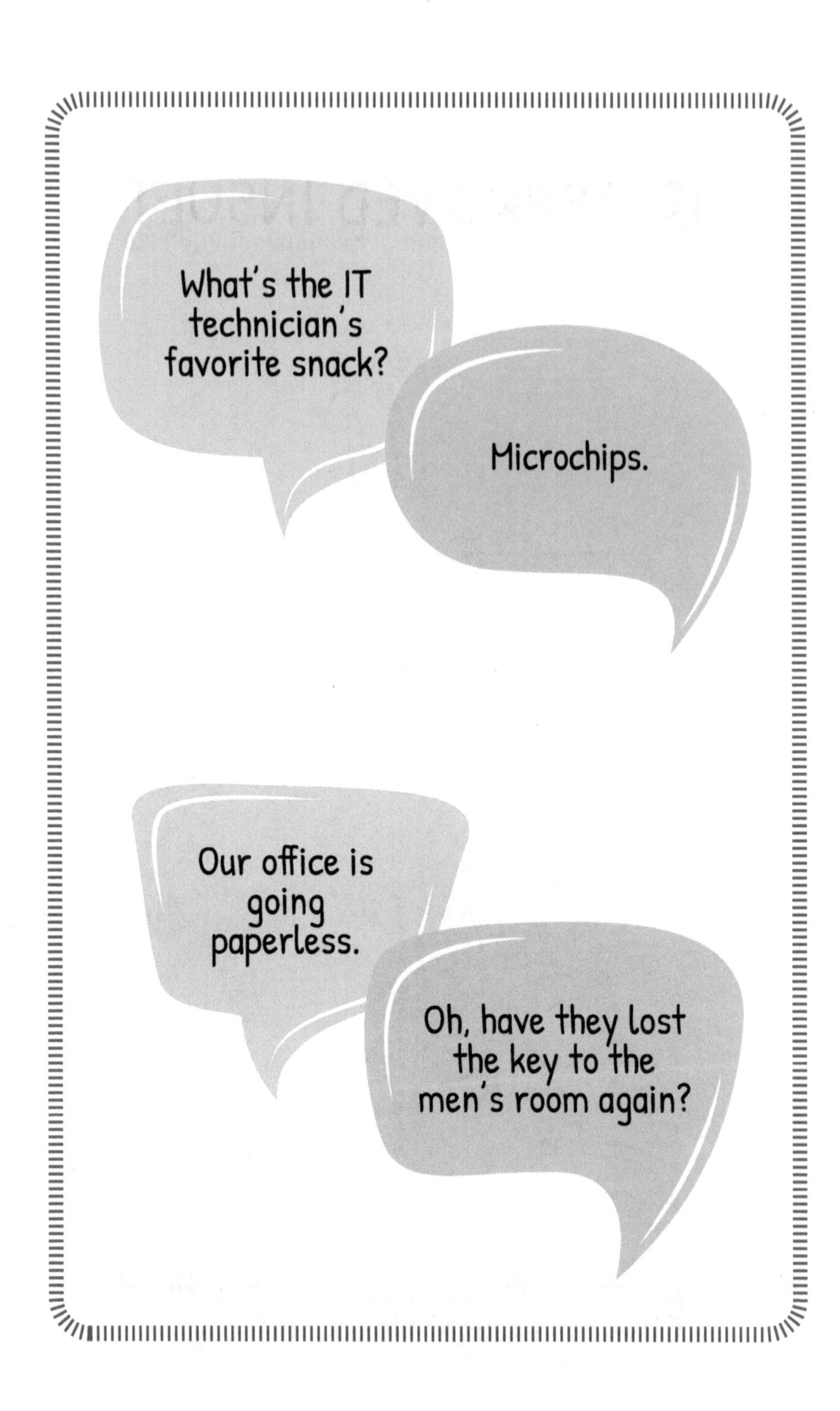
What's the IT technician's favorite snack?
Microchips.
Our office is going paperless.
Oh, have they lost the key to the men's room again?

THE WALLPAPER PRANK

The great thing about technologies like airdropping and BlueTooth is that you can very easily and quickly get a file from a mobile device onto a computer system.

Why does that matter? Well, make sure you have a library of the most ridiculous pictures you can find from the internet saved on your phone, and then bide your time in the office...

Then, the next time one of your colleagues leaves their computer unlocked for even just a minute or two—to go and take a call, print a document, grab a cup of coffee, whatever it might be—you can pounce.

Track down one of the pictures in your phone library, then wirelessly ping it onto their computer and set it as their desktop wallpaper.

There's no time-consuming connecting of cables here, so this should only take a minute or so. You can be in and out in seconds, and no one will know. In fact, if you do it subtly enough, no one might even know that you've done anything at all...

"Did you see that email I sent you?"

#5
HR-APPROVED INSULT

"Intelligence and ingenuity run in his family, you know. It's just a shame he runs faster."

Why was the astronaut a terrible typist?
He kept on hitting the space bar.
What's a photocopier's favorite food?
Paper jam.

THE PAPERCLIP TRICK

Do you have the one person in the office who's always picking up after everyone else? Always complaining about messes and trash? Always having a go about dropped this and forgotten that?

This is a prank with them in mind.

Leave a paperclip on the floor by their desk. They'll undoubtedly spot it. And pick it up. And complain about it. But little do they know, this paperclip wasn't dropped accidentally...

Lay a trail of paperclips all around the office, just far enough apart from one another so that it isn't an obvious trail—just enough to make it seem like someone accidentally dropped one or two while they were walking around. Make it look like, say, they were carrying a box of paperclips and didn't realize they were falling out as they went. Only, none of that has happened.

When your chosen victim spots the first clip, they will undoubtedly spot the second. And when they stoop down to pick that one up, they'll spot the third. Then the fourth. And then the fifth.

How many will they pick up before they realize that they're being sent on a Hansel and Gretel-style trail of breadcrumbs—or rather paperclips—all around the office, desk to desk? Will they pick them all up? Will they give up before the end? Place your bets now...

OFFICE WISDOM

#6
HR-APPROVED INSULT

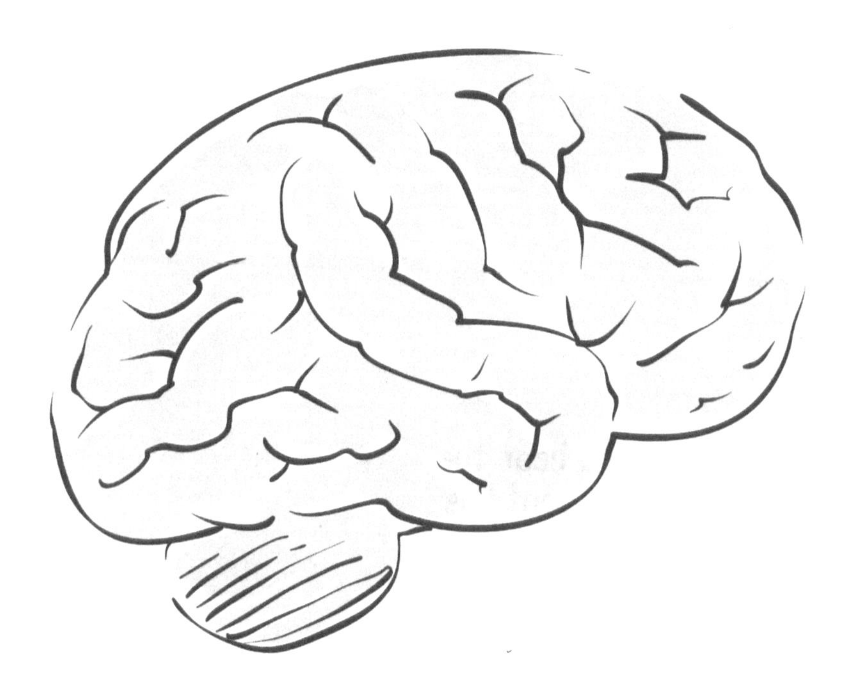

"His brain is working overtime.
It's just a shame he left at 2 o'clock."

What did the folder say to the paper?
I've got you covered.
Did you hear the office plant has been promoted?
Yeah, that's real career growth.

OFFICE PRANKS

THE POST-IT NOTE PRANK

There's always someone in the office whose idea of organization is to stick sticky notes up around their desk or cubicle.

All you need to do to pull a prank on them is to keep adding notes to their collection, with jobs and tasks written on there that they have no business doing.

"Finish the report." "2pm meeting, don't forget." "Jane will be off tomorrow, remember." (This works especially good if there isn't actually anyone called Jane in the office or in their email contacts!)

Every time they're not looking—or even before they arrive in the morning, or while they're in a meeting or out for lunch—just wander over and add another note into the mix.

"Tires rotated Thursday." "Transport strikes tomorrow!!" "Lunch lady retirement due." Write whatever you want on there, and just see how much confusion you can cause!

(Bonus points for getting their handwriting just right...)

OFFICE WISDOM

"I've been doing some crunches before work.

Cap'n and Nestle, mainly."

#7
HR-APPROVED INSULT

"I guess it's better to stay silent and worry people think you're a fool than open your mouth and remove all doubt."

I've got a really good Microsoft Office joke.
Word.
How was your date with the new guy in admin?
Oh, he ticks all the right boxes.

OFFICE PRANKS

THE PEN POT PRANK

Isn't it annoying when you're writing down a quick note—say, midway through a meeting, or while you're on a call to someone—and your pen runs dry?

Yeah, it's really annoying. In fact, it's so annoying, that it would be just the kind of thing that would get other people angry, right...?

This one takes a bit of long-term preparation.

Whenever a pen runs out in the office—yours, someone else's, you spot a discarded one in the waste paper bin, whatever the circumstances—keep it to one side. Within a few weeks, you should have a fair collection, depending on how much you and your workmates are writing things down these days.

Then, once you have enough, select your victim. Preferably, someone who has a pot of pens readily available on their desk. Then, when they're busy doing something else or away from their desk for lunch, say, sneak over and switch their collection of working pens for all the dud pens you've collected!

All you have to do then is sit back, wait for them to take a call, and watch the chaos unfold. "Sure," they say into the receiver, "I can do that. Can I just take your number, and I'll let you know as soon as possible? Let me just get a pen..."

8:59am on a work-from-home day,
9:00am on a work-from-home day

#8
HR-APPROVED INSULT

"I'm not saying they're a bad at their job.
I just mean they're not good at THIS job."

Did you hear about the paper airplane I made that didn't fly?

Yeah, it's stationery.

Why did the coffee machine talk to HR?

It had trouble espressoing itself in the office.

THE DONUT PRANK

You've treated your colleagues to a tray of donuts and left them in the break room. You're the toast of the office. Only, one of the donuts is a dud.

Buy a set of filled donuts of whatever flavor you like. Jelly, custard, chocolate, whatever. On top of that, though, buy yourself a plain donut, with no filling at all. Then, get a squeezy bottle of your favorite condiment—ketchup or mustard will work well—and, like the trained pastry chef you aren't, squeeze a healthy dollop of savory sauce into the odd donut out.

Then you can either deliberately hand this particular donut over to whoever you wish to prank, or—this might be more fun, actually—you could always hide it among all the others and wait for it to be discovered, Russian roulette style.

So long as it's not your boss who ends up with a mouthful of mustard rather than strawberry jelly, it should be all in good humor ... right?

"Nothing ruins a Friday more than realizing it's only Tuesday."

#9
HR-APPROVED INSULT

"They have a brain like quicksilver. At –40°F."

My pen's just been promoted over me!
I guess it has all the write skills?
Do you know what a clean office desk is a sign of?
Yeah. A cluttered desk drawer.

THE FAMILY ALBUM PRANK

Do you know coworkers who like to keep photographs of their loved ones around their desk?

If so, it's the perfect opportunity for a prank.

Make sure you arrive to the office before them, and come armed with a handful of the most bizarre photographs you can find. Print them off the internet, cut them out of magazines or catalogs—whatever you need to do to find the best (i.e., worst) photographs of bizarre-looking people in bizarre-looking situations that you can find.

Then, go to work swapping over all your coworker's photos. That picture of their mother and father? Hidden behind Al and Peggy Bundy. The picture of their kid at Summer Camp? Switch it for Wednesday Addams. Their brother on his yacht? Swap it for Sinbad.

How long before they spot the change? Could you make it to lunchtime without being rumbled? Bonus points if you make it to 5 o'clock—and you win the game if you make it to the end of the week!

OFFICE WISDOM

"The boss told me to have a good day, so I went home."

#10
HR-APPROVED INSULT

"Let's just say when it was raining brains, they carried an umbrella."

I just tried to call the admin department, but they're all engaged.
Oh, give them my congratulations!
Why did you leave your last job?
The company relocated. They just didn't tell me where they went.

THE GIFT WRAP PRANK

Who doesn't like presents, eh?

You can either wait until Christmas or your coworker's birthday to pull this one, but to be fair, it would work just as well on an otherwise dull and dreary Monday!

Sneak into the office early, armed with some garish wrapping paper. Then, you can do one of two things.

On the one hand, you can wrap up something on your colleague's desk that they already own and know they own, like a computer mouse and a mouse pad, and leave it on their desk as if it's the most thoughtful present imaginable.

Or, you can go crazy. Wrap EVERYTHING.

Their stapler, their chair, their coffee mug. Their lanyard, their keycard, their pencil case. Their phone, their computer monitor, their CPU. Go wild, cover everything—and then just wait for them to arrive...

OFFICE WISDOM

#11
HR-APPROVED INSULT

"He could hide his own Easter eggs."

Tell me, what do you think you could bring to this office?
Donuts?
The new guy just threw milk at me in the break room!
How dairy!

THE BALLOON POP PRANK

Wait until your coworker's birthday, then leave a couple of balloons on their desk as a fun and jokey celebration of their big day.

At some point that morning, go over and strike up a random conversation, and idly start playing with the balloons.

"Hey, I wonder how much it would take before one of these popped," you say casually, before starting to gently push and squeeze one of the balloons to see how far you can push it before it bursts.

With any luck—or with a little coaxing—your colleague will take up the other balloon and start playing your daft challenge themselves.

Eventually, you push your balloon too far and it bursts. You jump, everyone laughs, it's all a big joke. You colleague does the same—pushing the balloon as much as possible, until it pops.

It's at that point, of course, that they discover you handed them that balloon because that was the one you filled with confetti and glitter before you blew it up...

Me wondering why I have a bad back.

#12
HR-APPROVED INSULT

"It is impossible to underestimate you."

The office clock just went back four seconds.
That's funny, I thought all the donuts were gone.
Did you hear about the guy who just got a job at Old MacDonald's farm?
Yeah. He's the new CEIEIO.

OFFICE PRANKS

THE EMAIL PRANK

Everyone in the office knows everyone else's emails, of course. So this is your opportunity to take your coworker's email and sign it up to as many ridiculous newsletters and freebie websites as possible.

Track down the daftest, most outlandish deals and websites you can, and get their email signed up to them right away.

Daily motivation sites. Daily quote-of-the-day sites. Tourist attraction websites in completely different countries.

Hey, you name it, get them signed up to it.

Then, all you have to do is sit back and wait for the email floodgates to open—from all around the world and from the most bizarre and unexpected websites imaginable!

(Don't go too off the wall with those websites, of course. We don't want to have to get HR involved after all...)

OFFICE WISDOM

"I was told to start this presentation with a joke, so this first slide is my last paycheck."

#13
HR-APPROVED INSULT

"There's no beginning to his talents."

Why do birds sing in the morning?
They don't have to go to work.
Who are the two new guys at the window?
Kurt and Rod.

OFFICE WISDOM

"I got a job in
a paperless office.
It was fine until
I went to
the restroom."

#14
HR-APPROVED INSULT

"To save time, I'm going to give you an extension on this project now before you've started."

We need someone who's brave enough to make their own decisions for this role.

Oh now, do you think that's me or not?

This is the third time you've been late this week, do you know what that means?

It's Wednesday.

THE ZOOM GAME

When you're working from home, Zoom meetings can get a little boring. So why not spice things up with a little game you can either play on your own or get your workmates involved (remembering to leave one or two of them in the dark...)

Next, decide on a topic. Tim Burton movies. Taylor Swift songs. Queen lyrics. Whatever you choose, it's up to you (and whoever else, if anyone, you let in on the gag) to drop as many of them as possible into your meeting.

You score a point for each one you can seamlessly work into the conversation, or the post-presentation Q&A—or heck, even into the text of your own presentation.

Will anyone catch on? Will anyone else notice that you're picking and choosing your words somewhat more carefully than normal? The subtler you do it, the less likely you are to get found out...

When you take an extra 10 minutes for your lunch break

#15
HR-APPROVED INSULT

"He's the reason things have warning labels."

Can you work this weekend?
Yeah, I think so, but I might be a bit late if that's okay?
Sure, when can you get here by?
Monday.

OFFICE PRANKS

THE VIRTUAL BACKGROUND PRANK

Fair play to the people who came up with Zoom and Skype and Teams and all the other video-conferencing tech we use more frequently than ever in this post-pandemic world: they knew that things would be a lot more interesting if we were allowed to choose our own backgrounds.

Instead of just blurring your background out, though, you can have a little fun with it and see if anyone notices.

A good way to do that is to use your computer's ability to take a grab of the screen. Using the camera, take a screenshot of you standing in the background, behind your work-from-home desk, looking at your chair. Then, set this picture as your Zoom background—so that in true *Inception*-like style, you will be casually chatting away while looking at yourself.

Bonus points if you can make the background look like you're confused or pleased to see yourself—or if you can arrange it just so, so that it looks like background you is somehow interacting with your Zoom screen self. Like rubbing your shoulders or patting you on the head.

Will anyone notice?

Well, maybe if we had better coffee in the office
we'd have better productivity.

#16

HR-APPROVED INSULT

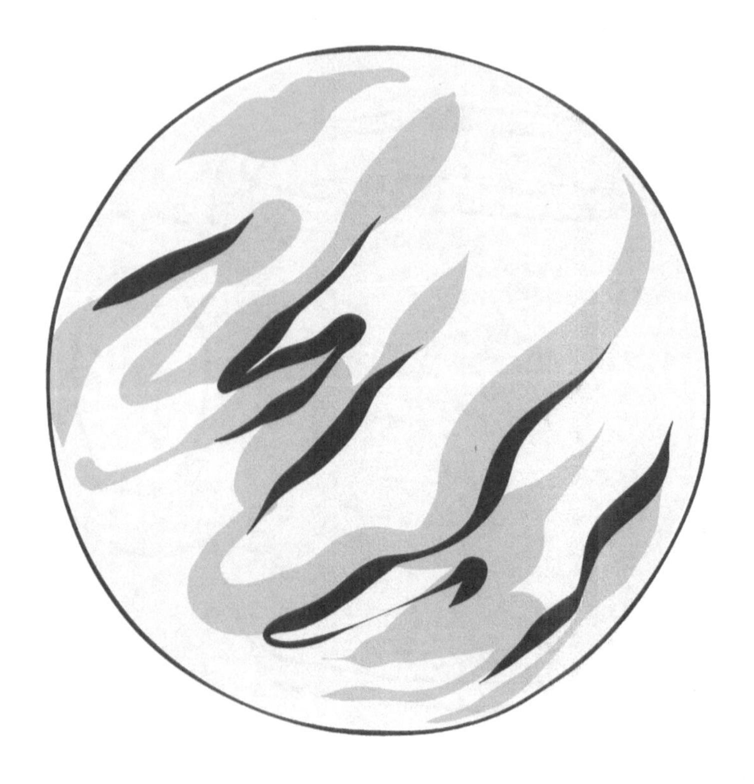

"He's as sharp as a marble."

What's the computer technician's favorite horror movie?

Stephen King's *IT*.

The boss says I'm a great motivator.

Yeah, everyone has to work twice as hard whenever you're in.

OFFICE PRANKS

THE HELIUM BALLOON PRANK

Ever since Stephen King's *IT* arrived on the scene, helium balloons have taken on a rather more sinister edge. Which makes them the perfect thing for a prank!

Track down some helium balloons, and hide them in drawers and cupboards all over your office. Your co-worker's desk. The file cabinet. The kitchen cupboards. The microwave. Inside the photocopier.

Hide as many of them as you can, in as many different places as you can.

Will they all be discovered by the end of the day? Or is this one of those things where people will still be finding the odd one weeks after the original prank?

Oh, and bonus points if you have an office with high ceilings... The higher the better, because there's no chance anyone's getting a helium balloon down without a ladder in some places!

"The best thing about deadlines is how quickly they go by."

#17
HR-APPROVED INSULT

"It's impressive how you manage to remain so confident."

There's no such thing as problems, only opportunities.

Well in that case, I've got a serious opportunity with the boss.

How many IT techs does it take to change a light bulb?

None, they said that's a hardware problem.

OFFICE PRANKS

MUTE PRANK

During the pandemic, when we were all just getting used to working from home and Zooming with one another rather than sitting around the same table in the office, one phrase kept on cropping up more than any other. "You're on mute!"

How many times did someone try to pipe up in an online meeting, only to begin talking while their microphone was still set to silent? Well, although we're all a bit better versed in online meeting tech these days, how about we go back to those good old days?

Next time you're on a Zoom meeting, tell someone who is speaking that their microphone is on mute—even when it isn't. They'll try to change it, but tell them again that they're on mute. Then tell them again. And again.

And again.

How long will they be able to stand it? How confused will they get? Hey, bonus points if they try to fix things by raising the volume of their voice...!

OFFICE WISDOM

"Never wear soft shoes in the office. That way you'll always be out of your comfort zone."

#18
HR-APPROVED INSULT

"I'll give your suggestion all the attention it deserves."

The new boss is a bit of a control freak.
Oh, he hasn't told me that yet.
How well do you handle stress?
Define "well..."

THE SEED BED PRANK

Hey, remember at school when we all had to grow cress in yogurt pots? It might be a long time ago (if you can remember doing it—or if you did it at all, of course) but one take away from that is that cress grows everywhere.

So, if you have a colleague who's heading off on vacation for a while, this makes a great opportunity for a prank!

Take the frontispiece off their computer keyboard—or, for a really sadistic twist, just remove the keys for the letters in GRASS or CRESS.

Then, tip in a few moist cress seeds. Those things grow so easily everywhere, that within a few days there'll be fresh green growth poking up above the letters on the keyboard.

And by the time they get back, there might be enough sprouting out of there to garnish an egg sandwich!

OFFICE WISDOM

"The jokes you hear in the elevator are always the best because they work on so many levels."

#19
HR-APPROVED INSULT

"Well, what you see as low self-esteem,
I see as you knowing limitations."

Are you enjoying the work here?
Sure. It's the people I don't like.
Why'd that guy put sunglasses on the drinks machine?
He wanted to make the water cooler.

THE CALENDAR PRANK

It's coming to the end of the year, and it's time to pick out a few Secret Santa gifts.

When that time comes, it's easy to fall into the trap of just getting everyone the same old usual things. Socks. Gloves. A scarf. A nice pen. A new coffee mug. Some stationery.

But do you have that one colleague who deserves something extra special? For them, here's an idea...

Track down one of those websites online where you can print your own calendars by uploading photographs of your choice. Some of them only cost a few dollars and let you upload a full year's worth of images, one for every month of the new year.

You could do anything you want with this, of course, but how about making this extra special colleague's extra special present all about them?

Use their photo ID picture, their lanyard ID picture, their copier card ID picture. Track down whatever awful, sterile, badly-lit, office-based images of them you can find, and upload them all to the website. Once you have a whole year's worth—twelve pictures in all—you're good to go!

Hey, you could even set this prank up across the entire year, taking the photos yourself on your phone, before staging the big reveal at Christmastime....

Zoom meeting cameras on,
Zoom meeting cameras off

#20
HR-APPROVED INSULT

"Has anyone told you you're doing a good job today? No? Oh. Fancy that..."

Why do Java programmers always wear glasses?
Because they don't C#.
Why have you brought a ladder to work?
I want to take myself to the next level.

THE LOG-ON MUSIC

Computers these days let you change everything. From the background wallpaper on your home screen to the sound you hear when you receive an email, practically everything is customizable.

So, next time your colleague wanders off from their desk and leaves their computer unattended, go into their settings and change their log-on jingle to whatever sound file you wish.

Track down an MP3 of a foghorn from the internet, or take a music file, an audio snippet from a movie you like, an animal's call, or whatever nonsense sound effect you wish, and set it as their log-on music.

Then, make sure you're in place early the next day so that you can see them casually type in their password, and await the big reveal...

OFFICE WISDOM

"Never tell jokes in your Zoom meetings when you're working from home. The boss doesn't find them remotely funny."

#21
HR-APPROVED INSULT

"He's so far behind, he thinks he's in front."

Why have they promoted that carpenter?!
He did great at all the board meetings.
Would you consider yourself motivated?
Absolutely, I can't wait for 5pm.

OFFICE PRANKS

THE OFFICE CHAIR SPRAY

You've no doubt seen those movies on the internet where someone straps an airhorn to someone's chair in an office, and as they sit on it, the horn blares and the colleague doubtless goes flying over backwards.

It's a fun prank, but it's a little too wild for most workspaces. The mechanism that triggers it, though, can be put to all kinds of good uses.

Instead of an airhorn under someone's desk, how about an air freshener, or a can of Febreeze? A faint spritz of something pleasant every time they sit down is far more pleasant than a shocking, blaring airhorn, after all.

But then again, a faint spritz of something pleasant isn't very prankish, is it?

So how about using that spritz bottle with something else inside of it?

Vinegar might be a good shout. It's a lot more acrid smelling, but it's clear and so might easily go unnoticed in a transparent bottle, hidden away in the gloom under a desk.

How long before your colleague notices something is amiss?

How long before they figure out that they are the one filling the office with a foul stench every time they sit down or shift in their chair?

Or will they prove too polite or too embarrassed to say anything at all—least of all, to cry foul play?

(With emphasis on the foul there...)

"Okay, so who wrote 'Get rid of the suggestions tub?'"

#22
HR-APPROVED INSULT

"He's a very handsome guy. I guess there really is beauty in simplicity."

Why did the boss start taking piano lessons?
He wanted to be seen as a real key player.
How do you know the manager is stressed?
Whenever they tell you it's all under control.

THE SCREEN FLIP

It's a classic prank. But oddly, it's one that many people don't know how to do—and even more people don't know how to fix.

Hidden away among the customization settings on a standard computer will be the option to rotate the screen. This helps to deliver presentations to audiences, among all sorts of other practical applications—but in an office, it's best used just for pranks.

As soon as a colleague's computer goes unattended, sneak into their preferences and activate the screen flip. (If speed is of the essence, make sure you know how to do this before you take a seat at their desk!)

Once the deed is done, retake your seat, and sit back and watch them try to figure out (a) what's happened, and (b) how to put the dratted thing back the right way!

OFFICE WISDOM

#23
HR-APPROVED INSULT

"Well, at least you've clearly written this yourself."

Did you hear that the marketing manager has dumped their long-term boyfriend?

Yeah, they were annoyed by the lack of engagement.

The coffee drinkers are the worst gossips in the office.

I know, they really love to spill the beans.

THE FAKE UPDATE

Next time your computer crashes or has a long update, take a screenshot of the waiting screen.

Or, alternatively, just type "update screen" into a search engine, and save the photo.

Next time your workmate is away from their desk, upload this screenshot to their computer, and just leave the picture open on their screen. That way, it should fill the entire screen, with nothing else floating around on top of it (as would happen if you made it their wallpaper). No, just open the file, and leave it be.

Chances are, they'll think their unattended computer has decided to update itself in their absence, and they'll have to wait until it's finished doing so before they can crack on with anything else!

How long before they smell a rat and realize the "update" is nothing of the sort?

OFFICE WISDOM

#24
HR-APPROVED INSULT

"You know, I don't care what everyone else here says, I think you're good at your job."

What did the marketing team get you for your birthday?
A bottle of brand-y.
As I begin this presentation, we all have something in common...
...you don't know what I'm going to say, and neither do I.

THE PACKING BOXES PRANK

Deliveries are arriving at busy offices day in, day out.

And there's always that one delivery guy who doesn't quite follow the right instructions and just leaves his delivery wherever he wants, right?

And for that matter, there's always that one coworker who gets super annoyed about the delivery guy not following instructions too, right?

Oh, it's like a marriage made in prank heaven.

So. First, find a few large, bulky-looking cardboard boxes.

Then, you want to subtly tape or glue them together, so that rather than a large pile of heavy-looking boxes, you have just a single, pasted-together mass of boxes that can be lifted up as one. The trick is, though, to make this pile of boxes as light as possible, so trim off any excess you can.

Next, leave this heavy-looking-but-not-actually-heavy-at-all glued-together pile of empty boxes by your nitpicking prank victim's desk.

Then, all you need do is wait for them to arrive, see the error, and decide to take matters into their own hands and tidy the mess up themselves.

The fact that all these boxes move as a single unit should be shocking enough for the prank to work. But if done correctly, your prankee should expect the boxes to be heavy and put a little effort into lifting one of them up, only to find it weighs nothing at all—and in doing so, fling the whole mass high into the air!

OFFICE WISDOM

"If you don't like taking the elevator up to your office, you can take steps to avoid them."

#25
HR-APPROVED INSULT

"He continually inspires other people to think about who they talk to here."

I never thought I'd be the kind of person to get up early and exercise before work...

...and I was right.

Rolling out of bed on Monday morning is easy...

...it's getting up off the floor afterward that's the hard part.

OFFICE PRANKS

THE PENNY TRICK

This is a prank that has been doing the rounds for decades, but it's always worth a revisit.

Once the work of con artists and street hustlers, the penny trick simply involves gluing or otherwise sticking down a penny, a nickel, or some other low-value amount of money to a person's desk—or, even better, to the floor below it.

Once they notice it, they'll understandably try to pick it up. And the stronger you've glued it down, the longer they're going to be there trying to free it...

And hey, while we're at it—why stop at a penny? Why not glue a coffee cup down, or a stapler, or an old ID card? So long as you're not doing any permanent damage (perish the thought), the list of versions of this prank is endless...

"Not working from home has its advantages too, I guess."

#26
HR-APPROVED INSULT

"Sure, I can give you a reference!
I'll do anything to help you move on from here."

I told HR I've been finding it hard to get motivated first thing.

Oh, the old Monday morning problem?

No, no, it happens every day now.

THE MOUSE PAD PRANK

These days, many people are working on laptops fitted with state-of-the-art trackpads. Swiping from page to page and window to window is a heck of a lot easier than constantly waving a mouse around and pointing and clicking, after all.

But for those of you whose offices are still in the mouse-and-a-mousepad world of modern technology, this classic prank is perfect.

While your colleague is away from their desk, place a piece of clear tape over the sensor of their mouse. When they return, they'll try to pick up where they left off, only to find their mouse not quite as responsive as it was barely a minute or two ago!

They might try shaking and clicking and tapping and knocking it, but with the transparent sliver of tape the only thing causing the issues, it might be a while before they work out precisely what's wrong...

OFFICE WISDOM

#27 HR-APPROVED INSULT

"If you offered him a penny for his thoughts, you'd still have that penny next week."

Hard work always pays off later.
Ah, yes, but laziness pays off straight away.
He's so good at multitasking.
You're right, he can waste time and procrastinate at the same time.

THE FAKE BIRTHDAY

Isn't it lovely when it's someone's birthday in the office and everyone gathers around their cubicle to sing "Happy Birthday" and hand them a delicious cake?

It's even more lovely when you've arranged the entire thing knowing full well that it isn't actually their birthday!

Whether you let your coworkers in on this joke or not, the idea is to make your prank victim squirm with awkwardness while you all approach out of nowhere—candlelit cake in hand—already a line or two into "Happy Birthday."

Are they going to let you all down by telling the truth? Or are they going to keep their mouth shut, let you finish the song, and hide their secret for the sake of some free cake?

And more importantly, when do you let them know that you're all in on it?

OFFICE WISDOM

#28
HR-APPROVED INSULT

"He has a real knack for stating the obvious with a sense of discovery."

OFFICE WISDOM

If you'll like to take a look at me resumé...

...you'll see a lot of things I hope you don't ask me to do.

I've got lots of jokes about how lazy the bosses are...

...but none of them really work.

"I'd be a great
morning person
if the morning
started at 1pm."

#29
HR-APPROVED INSULT

"You researched all of this yourself? Well, at least you had fun."

What's the worst thing that can happen on a Friday morning?

Realize that it's actually Thursday.

Don't you just hate people who answer questions with other questions?

Oh, what's more annoying than that?

THE PACKING PEANUTS PRANK

Okay, we're nearing the end here, so let's go all out for this last prank!

Who doesn't love playing with packing peanuts, eh? And if you have a ready supply of them in your office—after a large delivery is the perfect time to enact this one—then set them aside to use for the perfect prank.

Use the peanuts to fill up every drawer, every vessel, and every container you can imagine that your prank victim is going to use in a day. From the drawers in their desk to their mug in the cupboard to the paper tray of their printer, get those polystyrene peanuts absolutely everywhere.

Then, all you need do is sit back and watch chaos rain—for all the rest of the day!

The longest hour of the day
is the one between 4:59 and 5:00.

#30
HR-APPROVED INSULT

"No, you're not the dumbest person here.
But you'd better hope they don't leave."

CONCLUSION

You're no lamebrain with a head like frozen quicksilver.

You're not a sandwich short of a picnic basket, that's for sure. And you're not a card short of a full deck, or an ace short of a trick—that's because you've made it to the very end of your *HR-Authorized Ways To Tell Coworkers They're Dumb*!

Hopefully these last hundred pages or so have contained more than enough jokes and japes to keep you thoroughly entertained—whether that's with sage office advice, a one-liner or a quick back-and-forth punning joke, or a prank that is destined to be deployed the next time you're at a loose end in the office.

And along the way too, hopefully you've picked up a few ways to tell someone they're dumb, without actually telling them they're dumb. Hey, who knows when those might next come in handy!

But be careful what you do with this information, of course—and with this book. Don't go letting too many people sneak a peek at it, because the last thing you want is to be on the receiving end of an HR-approved insult.

Or, for that matter, a desk full of packing peanuts...

Made in United States
Troutdale, OR
12/09/2024